Cleaning and maintaining modern and antique firearms

Cleaning and maintaining modern and antique firearms
- a concise guide

This book deals with all aspects of the cleaning and maintenance of the most commonly encountered types of sporting firearms. It gives practical advice distilled from the author's 50 years' experience in shooting sports. Cleaning materials and other consumables are discussed in detail, as are the tools and implements necessary to maintain a gun's condition, reliability and value. The specialist techniques needed for cleaning and maintaining every type of firearm are described, as are those for dealing with ancillary equipment.

by Bill Harriman
Photography by Chantel Taylor

The British Association for Shooting & Conservation

Quiller

Copyright © 2019 Bill Harriman

First published in the UK in 2019
by Quiller, an imprint of Quiller Publishing Ltd

British Library Cataloguing-in-Publication Data
A catalogue record for this book is available from the British Library

ISBN 9781846892776

Cover image by Chantel Taylor

Printed in the Czech Republic

Quiller
An imprint of Quiller Publishing Ltd
Wykey House, Wykey, Shrewsbury, SY4 1JA
Tel: 01939 261 616
E-mail: info@quillerbooks.com
Website: www.quillerpublishing.com

Contents

The Author

Bill Harriman is Director of Firearms at the British Association for Shooting and Conservation (BASC). Before joining the Association in 1991 he worked in Birmingham for a firm of auctioneers specialising in guns, arms and armour. From 1974 to 1991 he served in the Territorial Army (Royal Artillery and Royal Yeomanry), retiring with the rank of Captain.

He is one of a team of arms and militaria specialists for the BBC TV programme *Antiques Roadshow* since 1985. He is also a Fellow of the Society of Antiquaries of London and an honorary historical adviser to the Royal Armouries. He is also President of the Muzzle Loaders Association of Great Britain.

He is a professional member of the Chartered Society for Forensic Science and gives evidence in court on ballistic issues.

Bill collects infantry rifles (1830-1918), their ammunition and accessories. He also enjoys rough shooting, particularly with a muzzle loader. Outside of shooting Bill enjoys real ale, opera, painting model soldiers and playing snooker at his club in Chester. He lives in North Wales, is married to Janet and has two adult daughters, Annabel and Caroline.

Acknowledgements

The author would like to extend his gratitude to:
Mike Montgomery, for editing the book
Chantel Taylor for taking most of the photographs
Sarah East for the design

INTRODUCTION

I have been shooting since the early 1970s – that's nearly 50 years. I've been lucky to have had many people who have encouraged me and shared their knowledge with me. One person whose name sticks out is my late uncle, Herbert Butcher of Thorney near Peterborough. Uncle Herbert was a farmer who enjoyed his shooting and who recognised that his somewhat wayward nephew was developing a passion for it too. He taught me the safe use of firearms and how to look after them. One of his many maxims has always stuck in my mind. After a day's shooting, whether formal or rough, Uncle Herbert had a set routine of activities with a set order in which they were to be done. To remember this, I had to learn this little tick-list: 'Clean dog, feed dog. Hang game, clean gun and feed self'. No deviation was permitted from this regimen, even though you might be starved with hunger, numb with cold and dog-tired. Apparently, it had been handed down by Uncle Herbert's father, the legendary Great Uncle Joe whom it was not my privilege to know. It probably came from his father and so on.

It was an entirely logical sequence predicated on what needed to be done and the order in which it had to be executed. First, was looking after a faithful companion who had contributed to a successful day, the gundog. I have always considered that the care of another sentient being is a great basis for teaching responsibility to children. If engendered in childhood, it carries on into adult life. Next came respect for quarry, with the day's bag hung in a cool outhouse so that it did not spoil and be wasted.

Then came the process that this book is all about – the cleaning of your gun and equipment. Uncle used to delegate that task to me, not because he was lazy but because he knew that the best way to teach someone how to do something was to get them to do it. He was pushing at an open door, as I revelled in being able to handle the guns, which were otherwise off-limits. To this day, I can still remember the

The author shooting a newly made Purdey hammer gun in 2004

smells of fired paper cartridges and Rangoon oil. It was a heady aroma which will stay with me until I am carried out in a wooden overcoat. I learnt a lot about guns simply from being able to handle them. I also learnt to respect other people's property and return it to them in good order. Uncle Herbert's inspection was a tense time, for he was more meticulous than any Sergeant-Major with a recruit. I came to crave his approbation and when he professed some part to be still dirty, I felt I had failed not only him but myself as well. Only when all was as it should be and the guns put up in an old cupboard (no steel cabinets then) could I satisfy my inner youth with one of Auntie Margaret's hearty farmhouse teas.

The habit of cleaning a gun immediately after use has stayed with me today. It served me well during my time as a Territorial Army officer. My troop always had the cleanest personal weapons, having been made to clean them in any spare moment they had while on duty. In fact, I only ever charged one soldier in an 18-year career; he was a lazy scrub who had allowed his self-loading rifle to become red with rust. That negligence cost him his weekend R & R while he cleaned his rifle in the guardroom. I did this not because I was some tiresome martinet, but because all our lives might have depended on his rifle working. Your lives will never depend on your shotgun or stalking rifle firing, but your sport and enjoyment will. In any case a reliable firearm is a safe one.

We live in an era which has given us reliable, non-corrosive ammunition and excellent cleaning equipment. No longer are we at the mercy of mercuric primers and powders whose combustion products would rust the bore at the drop of a hat. For all that, we still need to clean our guns if we are to have absolute reliance in them. There is another dimension to this as well. When you clean a gun thoroughly, you really get to know it and that can only enhance your shooting. A well-maintained gun will keep its value and become something to hand on to the next generation.

This book is not just about preserving wood and metal; it's about preserving heritage too.

Bill Harriman
Director of Firearms, BASC
March 2019

SAFETY FIRST

Safety is just as important a consideration when cleaning or maintaining a firearm as it is when actually shooting it. I have heard lots of excuses long the lines of 'it went off when I was cleaning it!' Gun safety is an attitude of mind rather than slavish adherence to dogma. It is important not only to be safe but to be seen to be safe by others. Nobody should ever feel uncomfortable because of what you are doing with a gun.

I can remember, as a cadet in the Combined Cadet Force during the 1970s, having it drummed into me that it was vital to remove any element that allowed my rifle to function before cleaning it. That basic principle is still with me nearly five decades later. Remove the bolt and the rifle cannot fire; remove the magazine and there is no way that any ammunition can get into the chamber. That gives a 100% certainty that your firearm is safe to clean.

Your final action on finishing shooting must always be to ensure that your gun is unloaded before putting it in your slip for the journey home. Look down the barrel and make sure you can see daylight. If the light is poor, physically put your fingers into the chamber to prove to yourself that the gun is really empty. Show your companions that it is unloaded by pointing it at the ground and pressing the trigger. It is always reassuring to hear that 'click' which denotes an empty chamber. Count your cartridges too, preferably by using a wallet or other holder. Put fired cases back in the loops. That way you will know that you went out with nine cartridges and returned with two empty cases and seven unfired rounds. This is a bit fiddly with .22 or .17 rimfire rounds, as they are small, but an old plastic ammo box will allow this technique to be used as well.

When you get home, check the gun again before field-stripping it into the major component groups ready for cleaning. Never clean a gun that is not dismantled. A gun that is still assembled always presents the possibility that it still may contain ammunition. It goes without saying that guns should never be cleaned in the proximity of live ammunition. One that is in its major bits cannot possibly fire. You are safe and, more to the point, so are others around you.

Before cleaning a rifle, always remove the bolt and put it to one side. If the rifle has a detachable magazine, take that out as well and make sure it is empty. If it has a detachable floor-plate, remove it along with the magazine spring and follower too. If your rifle has a fixed integral magazine, like some Mausers, it is a good idea to make sure the magazine is empty and then put a bit of dowel or some other inert thing on the top of the follower. A child's wax crayon or piece of colouring pencil is handy and has the added advantage that it is brightly coloured.

It is especially important to remove the barrel of any magazine shotgun. Cartridges are not always easy to spot in a magazine. Tubular magazines are not possible to remove and extra care must be taken.

Removing the barrel not only makes cleaning it easier but is a fail-safe way of ensuring that the gun cannot go off.

Mainspring vice in use

Special care is needed when working on any spring. The only way to remove springs is with a mainspring vice; never be tempted to use pliers or Mole grips. Springs are very powerful and shatter easily if not supported when they are being removed, sending fragments, often sharp, flying around. Apart from breaking an expensive spring, you stand in real danger of being injured. Springs are best left to the professionals who have the right tools to deal with them safely.

The same applies to spring-powered air rifles. Their mainsprings are very powerful and it takes strength, practice and special tools to remove one safely. I once advised in a personal injury case where a chap had taken a springer to bits and the mainspring had flown out, blinding him.

A word on snap-caps and dummy cartridges. Always use snap-caps that do not look like real cartridges. Clear plastic ones could never be mistaken for the real thing. Neither could chromium-plated or aluminium ones. I am always wary of brass ones on the basis you sometimes get full length brass shotgun cartridges. Whatever you choose, NEVER use empty shotgun cartridges cases as snap-caps. I know of at least one fatality caused when a real cartridge was loaded in error by someone who thought it was an empty case.

Clear plastic snap-caps

Effective rifle cartridge dummies can be made by de-priming a spent case and drilling two small holes at right angles to each other through it. Make a full-length dummy bullet from a piece of dowel and stain it some bright colour (ink makes a good dye). Immerse the lower half of the case in brass black solution and then there will be no chance of mistaking the dummy for a live round. If your rifle is chambered for a military cartridge such as the .308WCF (7.62mm NATO), see if you can buy some purpose-made dummies from a militaria dealer or at an arms fair. These are often chromium-plated and have grooves filled with red paint around the sides. Purpose-made dummies exist for some sporting cartridges too.

When you have finished cleaning your gun, always make sure it is empty before putting it away. Check the chamber, point it in a safe direction and press the trigger. You can then be certain that it is safe to store. Always store guns with the springs in the released position. A spring that is left compressed may lose its temper over time and fail to work.

Lastly, a cautionary tale: I once heard that when a Firearm Enquiry Officer was checking guns during a renewal inspection, he found a live cartridge in the chamber of a shotgun. Fortunately, the only casualty on that occasion was the gun owner's certificate which was revoked in sharp order.

LEGAL CONSIDERATIONS

The Firearms Rules 1998 provide that every UK Firearm Certificate must carry the following statutory condition on it. (The same condition is applied to Shotgun Certificates, albeit that the condition does not refer to shotgun ammunition.)

(iv) **(a)** the firearms and ammunition to which the certificate relates must at all times (except in the circumstances set out in paragraph (b) below) be stored securely so as to prevent, so far as is reasonably practicable, access to the firearms or ammunition by an unauthorised person;

(b) where a firearm or ammunition to which the certificate relates is in use, or the holder of the certificate has the firearm with him for the purpose of cleaning, repairing or testing it or for some other purpose connected with its use, transfer or sale, or the firearm or ammunition is in transit to or from a place in connection with its use or any such purpose, reasonable precautions must be taken for the safe custody of the firearm or the ammunition.

It is a criminal offence to breach a condition on a certificate. If you do, you could be fined, go to prison or both. Irrespective of any punishment the court may award, it is a racing certainty that the police will revoke the certificate on the grounds that anyone who does not abide by this security condition must inevitably be a danger to public safety or the peace.

For most people, satisfying Part (a) of the condition (iv) will be by having a steel cabinet. Where the cabinet is sited is vital if the guns it contains are not to suffer damage. Moisture can penetrate a cabinet through the fixing holes if the wall is damp or if any damp-proof membrane is punctured during installation.

Steel cabinets may be prone to condensation if installed in cold, damp places. As there is no internal air circulation, guns are being stored in a cold, still and damp atmosphere which will result in corrosion very quickly. In such circumstances a low-powered lamp bulb may provide enough heat to raise the ambient air temperature and dispel any moisture. There are also products that claim to release protective vapours which protect the guns inside a cabinet. However, I have not seen any independent scientific verification of these claims.

Siting a cabinet in a place that is warm and damp-free is a fundamental requirement to avoid compromising your firearms maintenance regime.

Part (b) of condition (iv) tells a shooter what he must do when his firearm is in use or being cleaned or tested etc. The condition needs to be broken down into its operative phrases.

The first one is 'has with him'. This means that the certificate holder is in physical possession of the firearm.

Next, there must be a purpose which is connected to either its use or to one of the other stated purposes. Preferably such a link should be obvious but in the event of a prosecution, it would be for the Crown to prove that such a link did not exist. Lastly, the certificate holder must take 'reasonable precautions' for the firearm's safe custody. The last two words mean secure keeping.

For something to be reasonable in law, it must be reasonable in all of the individual circumstances. That means that what is reasonable for Jim, might not be reasonable for Sally in another situation. There is also a sense of middle-of-the road behaviour in the term. The precautions taken need not be excessively strict, but they may not be excessively lax either.

I have heard of numerous instances when an unannounced visit by the police has revealed a firearm or shotgun that is not in its cabinet. The inevitable excuse is always 'I had just left it out to clean it'. That is seldom believed and unhappiness generally follows.

If you are to convince a police officer or Firearms Enquiry Officer that you really were in the process of cleaning your gun, then the context around that needs to be credible. The gun needs to be dismantled for cleaning, the cleaning kit must be to hand and there must be a recent connection to the gun's use. It is no good claiming that you are cleaning a shotgun which is casually propped up behind the kitchen door, when your cleaning kit is still where it usually lives and the car's engine is stone cold, it not having been driven for some little time. The context is just not right.

People often allege that they have left out a gun because it is drying. That is a reasonable proposition as no gun should be put away in a wet state. The best solution would be to use a hair dryer but some people prefer the gentle heat from a plate rack, especially for the barrels. In such a case, dry off the stock/action and forend as best you can, before locking them in your cabinet. When the barrels have dried out on the plate rack, they can be exchanged for the other component groups. The component parts of a shotgun do not constitute a shotgun in law so you could never be accused of failing to take safe custody of one.

This does not work so well for rifles, because the relevant component part (bolt, barrel, action etc) is classed as a complete firearm in law. However, if you lock away part of your rifle and stay near to the other while it dries then I am sure that you can be said to 'have it with you' and no offence will be committed.

Drying wet shotgun barrels with a hairdryer

The upshot of all this is that you need to show that you were actually cleaning the firearm and that it was with you at the time. It is no good leaving the bits spread out on the kitchen table while you go out to the pub. Be sensible and do nothing that might cast doubt on an otherwise plausible explanation.

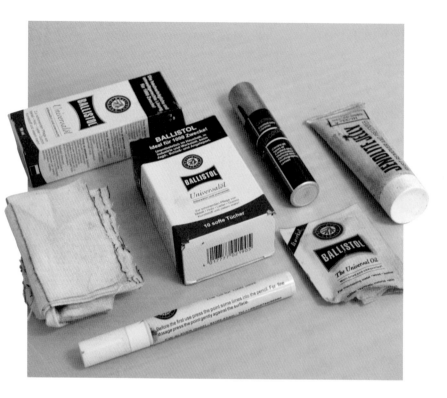

CLEANING MATERIALS

This chapter covers the consumables that are used for routine gun cleaning and maintenance. I deal with other products for more specialist applications elsewhere in the book.

It is common sense if using any volatile liquid to do so either outdoors or in a well-ventilated building. A small face mask might be appropriate too. Thin surgical gloves are a good idea when handling chemicals, where ordinary rubber washing-up gloves would be too bulky. Avoid getting oil or other fluids on sensitive areas of skin or in cuts.

IMPORTANT: The following two substances have no part in gun cleaning or maintenance as they are actively harmful to guns and their finishes.

Emery paper

Never be tempted to use emery paper – however fine – on a gun. Emery removes metal and will wipe out original finish and age patination in seconds. It leaves an abrasive residue which turns gun oil into grinding paste.

Spirit vinegar

This removes blued finishes very quickly. Indeed, from what I can ascertain, commercial de-bluing solutions contain a large proportion of acetic acid.

Oil

Oil has two functions in gun maintenance. Firstly, it lubricates moving parts and allows them to move freely and quickly against one another. This helps to reduce wear. Secondly, it protects against corrosion by forming a thin film which is impervious to the oxygen that causes rust.

There are many oils on the market described as being specially formulated for guns and which are claimed to have special properties. In my experience, this is simply marketing hype and a tin of what is described as 'Uncle Tom's Patent Gun Oil' is no more than an ordinary light oil with a craftily designed label intended to convince a prospective purchaser that this is the best lubricant for his gun. The price is also adjusted upwards accordingly.

All that is needed to lubricate a gun's mechanism and preserve against corrosion is ordinary light mineral oil. It is never a good idea to use car engine oil as this tends to be much more viscous and may impede the free movement of parts. In any case, oil of any variety tends to attract dust and other small particles. Eventually this creates a thick, sticky paste that may cause the gun's mechanism to seize up, particularly if it has not been used for some while. The thicker the oil, the more likely it will leave a gummy residue.

Some older shooters swear by what is known as 'Rangoon Oil'. Rather than having some magical property, this was no more than a light grade of mineral oil sold by the Rangoon Oil Company. By dint of effective marketing, this firm seems to have convinced much of the gun trade that this was the only oil worth having and you often see tins or bottles of it in old gun cases or advertised in gunmaker's catalogues.

Oil degenerates over time and, as evaporation of its more volatile elements occurs, begins to thicken. Old oil is always best avoided. You only have to look at the deposits on the neck of an old oil bottle or tin to see that it forms a thick gummy deposit as it dries. You don't want something like that in the mechanism of your gun.

Vegetable oils, such as olive oil, are perfectly good as lubricants. Indeed, vegetable oils were the only lubricants and metal preservatives available to firearms users before the widespread availability of mineral oils in the 19th Century.

Carrying an oily rag in your field cleaning kit is a good idea. Take a piece of cotton rag and put a few drops of oil onto it. Scrunch it up so that this becomes dispersed. Avoid too much oil; the rag does not need to be sopping with it, just oily to the touch. The oiled rag can then be put into a small container. An empty travel sweet tin is ideal, as is a small plastic food storage box.

Bore solvents

These help in the cleaning process by dissolving powder residues caused by combustion. These residues are baked on to the inside of the bore by high temperatures and pressures. Consequently, they become difficult to remove.

Chemical solvents are particularly useful if a large number of shots have been fired on a single occasion e.g. a round of clays. They are not always necessary for a small number of shots when large amounts of residue have not built up, e.g. after deer stalking. It all comes down to regular examination; if you can't seem to get a bore really clean, then try some solvent.

Many solvents contain some nasty chemicals and you should wear surgical gloves and neither eat nor drink while using them. Read the manufacturer's safety advice and abide by it.

Bore solvents are particularly useful for removing polythene wad deposits from shotgun bores. They reduce these to a slimy, grey-coloured substance that can easily be removed by a brush or cleaning patch. However, as many shoots now have an ecologically sound 'Fibre Wads Only' rule to prevent plastic waste littering the countryside, the need for chemicals to remove polythene fouling in shotgun barrels will eventually reduce.

Solvents are essential for rifles where metallic fouling has built up. When a bullet travels up a rifle's barrel, minute fragments of its jacket are scraped off by the rifling. The incredibly high pressures and temperatures instantly harden them, making them difficult to remove. If metallic deposits build up too much, they can affect the rifle's accuracy. The judicious use of solvents on a regular basis prevents this happening.

Black powder solvent

This is essential if you shoot a muzzle-loading gun or use black powder cartridges. In my experience it is the only substance that removes black powder fouling. Water on its own (whether hot or cold) cannot do this.

A wad of newspaper pushed through shotgun barrels will remove the worst of any fouling

Newspaper

This is very handy stuff. It will protect surfaces against accidental spillage of oils or chemicals during the cleaning process. It is also soft and will not scratch any gun or components laid on it. There are purpose-made gun cleaning mats on the market. To my mind, several sheets of newspaper are just as good and a lot more absorbent. In any case, a mat that is rolled up and reused may retain small, sharp particles in its weave that may scratch any gun laid on it. Newspaper can be thrown away after every use, eliminating this problem.

Newspaper is also useful for removing the worst of any really bad fouling from a shotgun barrel before cloth patches are used. A correct-sized piece, rolled into a ball can be pushed through the bore with a cleaning rod. The ink used on newsprint acts as a lubricant, so it goes through easily. A couple of pieces will normally push out the worst of any fouling.

Kitchen paper

This is also a useful and readily available cleaning resource that can be discarded after use. It is very absorbent and will remove excess moisture after shooting in the rain. When dampened, it is very good for removing mud and dirt from stocks, gun slips, ammunition belts and cartridge bags.

Rag

Running a rag cleaning patch through a firearm's bore serves two purposes. It not only absorbs any fouling loosened by solvents but also pushes any loose fouling out in front of it. It may also help to polish the bore.

Any cotton rag will do for cleaning. Avoid cloth made with man-made fibres as it tends to be less absorbent. A good source is old bed sheets or shirts. As these have been frequently washed, the cotton fibres will have lost most of the lint that adheres to them. That is one less source of material to get mixed in with the oil. Although rag tears easily, I always find it best to cut it to the precise size needed with scissors. Pre-cutting shotgun patches is a good idea. Trial and error will determine the size best for your bore of gun. It needs to be a tight fit but not so tight that it gets stuck in the bore. When you are happy with the dimensions of a cleaning patch, cut a template so that you can replicate them. I have never bought pre-cut shotgun patches. They appear to me to be an expensive way of buying cloth!

Flannelette

The British Army used to issue 'Four-by-Two' flannelette for cleaning .303 and 7.62 rifle barrels. It is still available to buy commercially. It is absorbent and has the advantage that a piece of suitable size for cleaning a rifle of approximately .30 cal (8mm) is delineated by the red strips on a roll of it.

Wooden cocktail sticks or toothpicks

Cocktail sticks or toothpicks are very useful for getting dirt out of relatively inaccessible spaces, such as the joint between the barrels and rib of a shotgun or the slots of screws. It is always amazing how much dirt accumulates in such places; the sharp points of these things will winkle it out without scratching the gun's finish. They are also very useful for depositing a small drop of oil on a precise spot. Wooden drinks stirrers sharpened to a point work equally as well. It is always worth grabbing a handful from a restaurant when the opportunity presents itself.

Steel wool

Steel wool soaked in meths used to clean a shotgun stock

Cabinet maker's grade steel wool (000 or 0000) is abrasive without being able to scratch steel or its finish. It is readily available from DIY shops and is inexpensive. If rust spots have formed, they can be easily and safely removed by using it. On older guns, it removes grime and rust without damaging attractive age patina. It is best soaked in light oil before use, as this helps to retain the rust particles as they are removed.

When a piece has become clogged with rust, it needs to be discarded in favour of a clean piece. Rust is very hard and becomes an abrasive in its own right if allowed to accumulate in the steel wool.

Boiled linseed oil

If your gun has a hand-oiled finish, this needs to be refreshed from time to time. A little oil rubbed into the stock using the ball of the hand will bring it to life and dissipate the dull look that oiled stocks develop after a while. A small amount goes a long way.

Touch-up gun blue

This is available as a paste or liquid. It works very well on small components but always looks thin and streaky when applied to larger areas. Follow the manufacturer's instructions for best results. This substance is invariably poisonous and the usual personal protection measures must be adopted.

Petrol

A small container of petrol is essential for rinsing parts, especially choke tubes. This needs to be done outside and well away from heat sources for obvious reasons. Make sure that the petrol will not dissolve the container you are proposing to use. Hard, polystyrene type plastic will be dissolved; glass, metal or polythene are fine. Try a tester on plastics and see if the surface starts to dissolve.

Dispose of any dirty petrol safely. As it is so volatile, small quantities evaporate easily if left outside in a container with a large surface area.

Household ammonia

This is used to neutralise the corrosive effect of firing older ammunition with mercuric primers. I used to shoot an old Soviet Mosin-Nagant rifle with ex-military ammunition. The bore would be red with rust almost by the time you had got back from the range. A wipe-out immediately after firing with an ammonia-soaked patch stopped any rust forming. Good ventilation is essential.

Methylated spirits

Meths is useful for a variety of jobs where it is necessary to dissolve accumulated grime. It is particularly effective in stock preparation when used in conjunction with fine steel wool. Use the same safety precautions as petrol, particularly where ventilation is concerned.

Car dashboard and trim restorer

This is very good on synthetic stocks. It not only provides a protective film but also restores colour and prevents fading.

Water-displacing aerosol spray

This does what it says and just disperses moisture. Although it is quite useful, it needs to be used in conjunction with a lubricant.

Protective silicone spray

This has been used to protect fishing tackle for quite a long time. It is equally good on guns, especially those which get wet regularly. A silicone cloth for your field maintenance kit is easily made using a rag and a few squirts of the spray on it.

Furniture restoration products

Scratch cover polish will help disguise all but the deepest scratches. These can be filled with coloured wax. These are good cosmetic solutions to the dings and scratches that a gun acquires in everyday use.

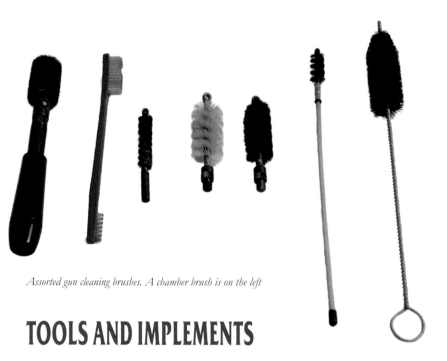

Assorted gun cleaning brushes. A chamber brush is on the left

TOOLS AND IMPLEMENTS

Cleaning rods for shotguns

Shotgun rods need to be robust; some of the flimsy wooden ones on the market are simply not up to the job. They will break during vigorous use. I prefer aluminium ones made in sections. They are tough and if two sets are bought they will make a rod long enough to clean the barrel of the longest musket or wildfowling gun. Being aluminium, they will not scratch or score the bore if they come into contact with it. It is a good idea to smear the threads with a little petroleum jelly or graphite grease after use. This makes them easier to unscrew. If you drill a 4 or 5mm hole in each section of an aluminium rod, a small piece of round bar can be inserted through the hole to act as a tommy bar if the sections become really hard to unscrew.

Attachments

A brush is needed to loosen stubborn fouling. I prefer phosphor bronze but stiff nylon or natural bristle is fine. The jag holds the cleaning patch. Again, I prefer a metal jag – brass or aluminium – because it is more durable. Avoid polythene ones as age plus repeated exposure to oil can make them brittle. Also, being soft, they can sometimes become impregnated with small particles of grit or metal which will scratch the gun's bore. The last attachment is a woolly mop for oiling the bore. This attracts dirt and grit so is best kept in a small tin to keep it clean.

It is always good practice to rinse the attachments from time to time in petrol. They need to be kept scrupulously clean to prevent them carrying foreign bodies into the bore.

Chamber brush

A purpose-made chamber brush is very useful. These tend to be made from brass wire with a short brush section and a handle. The brush part is much denser than a bore brush. It is a good idea to use a brush that is one bore size larger than your gun, e.g. I use a 12 bore in a 16 bore chamber. The extra tightness of fit really helps shift the dirt. Regular use of a chamber brush will keep your ejectors working smoothly, as empty cases are less likely to bind in a clean chamber. NB: these are often known as Payne-Gallwey brushes after the famous Victorian shooter who originally designed them.

Other brushes

- A toothbrush is an important part of any good cleaning kit. It will soon shift mud and other dirt from chequered areas and is handy for cleaning the area between the ribs and the barrels. Those sold by discount shops are perfectly adequate.

- A suede brush with brass bristles will serve a similar function. The metal bristles will also remove corrosion without scratching the steel or removing any finish.

- An artist's hog-bristle, square-tipped brush can be used to get into those less accessible nooks and crannies like the square slot for the rear lump on a side-by-side gun.

As with all brushes, when they become worn or dirty, throw them away and replace with new. That way you will not import dirty and abrasive material into your gun's action.

Cleaning rods for rifles

For me, the only effective cleaning rod for a rifle is a plastic-coated steel one with a rotating handle mounted on a ball race. I do not think brass or aluminium ones are durable enough to deal with the rigours of passing a thin rod up a small diameter bore. The same can be said for jointed ones; eventually, they break at the joint. It is far harder to pass a patched rod through the tight bore of a rifle than it is a shotgun.

Bore guides

Whatever rod you choose, always buy a bore guide to make sure it goes in exactly centrally. I think that guides are essential for rifles. Remember, the rifling controls the bullet's flight in the very early stages. Rifle bores are less forgiving than shotguns. A slight scratch in a shotgun's bore will probably have little effect on the pattern. The same scratch on a rifle bore may prevent it from ever being accurate again. The really critical part of any barrel is the crown. If that gets damaged then the rifle will not shoot straight until it is re-crowned.

Attachments

When choosing rifle brushes etc, most makers obligingly mark them with the calibre for which they are intended. Always stick to the correct size or one slightly smaller. For example a generic .30 calibre brush will accommodate a wide variety of cartridge chamberings, e.g. .308 WCF, 7.62mm, .303, .30-06 etc.

Again, I prefer phosphor-bronze bristles, preferably on a brass shaft. Bronze bristles are sometimes found mounted in twisted steel wire. They are fine but need to be checked regularly for rust. When a brush is worn or the bristles have lost their spring, chuck it away and replace it: they are not expensive. Your rifle is a precision tool; it behoves you to buy good quality cleaning implements to keep it in good fettle.

It is really important to use the right-sized jag combined with an appropriately-sized patch. It should offer some resistance as it passes up the barrel, but not too much. You do not want to get one stuck up the spout; getting it out is a job for a professional riflesmith.

Once the barrel is clean, it can be lightly oiled with the woolly mop. My remarks earlier about keeping it clean are especially relevant. You really don't want any potentially abrasive material in a rifle bore.

Chamber sticks

A chamber stick fulfils the same function in a rifle as a chamber brush does in a shotgun. It is made from wood with a gently pointed and slotted end. It extends well past the action and terminates in a square handle. A cleaning patch is centred in the slot and wrapped round the pointed part. That is inserted in the chamber and twisted so that the patch really cleans the surface of the chamber. It should make a squeaking noise while rotating if you are doing it right. Generally one size will fit every rifle in a major class of cartridges, e.g. .30cal or .22 centre fire.

Cleaning cradles for rifles

You don't really need to support a shotgun while it is being cleaned as its barrels are readily detachable. The same is not true for the majority of rifles, which need to be supported while the rod goes up the barrel. Being able to support the rifle's stock and forend during cleaning makes it less likely to get unsightly dings and scratches. It also means you can get a good grip on it. The American MTM cradle is ideal for someone on a budget. It has useful compartments to hold implements and cleaning material. As with anything, keep the cradle clean, otherwise you may scratch the stock if there is a bit of grit on its supports. At a pinch, a perfectly serviceable cradle can be improvised from a stout cardboard box with two Vs cut in opposite sides.

Assorted turn-screws. All have large handles to give a firm grip

Screwdrivers

Gunsmiths refer to these as 'turn-screws'. Domestic screwdrivers for DIY are WHOLLY UNSUITABLE for use on firearms. If you use one, you are likely to damage the screw slots of your gun. There is nothing more unsightly than mangled screw slots. It is an advert that the gun has been subject to dreadful bodging by an amateur.

It is important to keep screws properly tightened. A screw that has become undone may cause a malfunction and could be expensive to replace if lost. A good turn-screw has a short blade and a big handle for a really good grip. The blade needs to be ground to fit the screws it has to tighten or undo. The tip of the blade has to touch the bottom of the slot. One size definitely does not fit all. If you have several guns you will need several turn-screws.

I use American screwdrivers made by Grace or Wheeler with their blades/bits ground to match the screw slots I am working on. Grace screwdrivers are particularly good as they have squared handles which allow for a good grip. I have carefully ground the screwdriver blades on my Swiss Army knife for use in emergencies.

Pin punches

Again, buy proper engineering pin punches to deal with any pins that may work loose. Never be tempted to use one from a DIY supermarket. If your gun has rolled, hollow pins, you need a punch with a tiny dome on its tip. This fits into the hole in the pin and keeps pin and punch properly aligned during removal or seating.

Lyman offer a very useful small hammer that has a nylon face plus screw-in brass and steel ones. The handle is hollow and contains a useful brass drift. It is not large, but handy if you do need to hit anything hard during routine maintenance.

A hog-bristle artist's brush is very well suited for getting into the bolt locking lug recesses in the action body.

Choke keys

Interchangeable choke tubes always come with a key provided by the makers. In my experience, these are barely adequate. Choke tubes are quite fragile things and either they or the barrels or both can be damaged unless a well-fitting key is used to seat or remove them. I do not rate keys that only engage with two out of the four notches. Always go for a key that engages all four notches. That gives an even distribution of force which prevents potential distortion of the tube. Those keys which incorporate a small crank handle are superior to those which just have a bar. However, it is important not to use too much force when seating a choke.

There are also choke thread cleaning brushes. These are wound into the choke recess in the muzzle, the theory being that the rotating bristles remove any debris in the threads. Undoubtedly they work. However, I expect you could get the effect from an ordinary phosphor bronze brush on a section of rod twisted into the recess in the same manner. Certainly, it would be cheaper.

Other cleaning systems

Paradox cleaners

These are designed for shotguns. They have two-piece rods which screw together. The rods are covered overall with a fluffy material that looks like loft insulation, effectively they are a full-length barrel mop.

To use the Paradox, it is just inserted into the barrel and pushed through using a rotary motion. Several passes back and forth using the same technique will remove most fouling. When you are satisfied with the cleanliness of the bores, push the mop into a barrel until it protrudes from the muzzle. Attach the separate oiler, put a few drops of oil onto it and pull the mop out of the bore. After a bit of practice, you will find that this cleans the barrels very quickly.

Paradoxes are certainly very good after a relatively small number of fibre-wadded cartridges; they do not fare so well after a large number of plastic wads because of the plastic deposition in the bore. They are not really capable of removing lead deposits either.

I find the Paradox very handy for a quick clean immediately after shooting and keep one in my car. If my guns need a really deep clean, I wait until I get home and revert to more traditional methods.

Paradoxes are only offered in 12 and 20 bore sizes. I have found that the 12 will go through my 16 bore; in fact the slightly tighter fit makes for more effective cleaning. Presumably, the 20 bore size will go through a 28 as well.

Eventually the Paradox will become very dirty. It can be cleaned easily by rubbing washing-up liquid into the mop fibres, rinsing clean and then drying on a radiator or some other gentle heat source.

Paradox cleaners are not suitable for shotguns with black powder fouling. I once cleaned a black powder hammer gun with one and failed to get the highly acidic fouling off the mop. I then cleaned another gun with the dirty Paradox; two days later the bores were red with rust. I never made that mistake again.

Boresnakes

These are made for both rifles and shotguns. They comprise a weighted nylon pull-through attached to a tapering, thicker woven section

A Boresnake shotgun cleaner

which incorporates some phosphor bronze bristles. They tend to be calibre specific, although I find the 12 bore in a 16 bore barrel gets it really clean. I suspect the shotgun versions offer more flexibility than the rifle ones because of their greater diameters.

The Boresnake is very simple to use. The weight is dropped down the barrel of the gun. The slack of the pull through is wrapped around the hand for a few turns and then the whole shebang is pulled through the bore. As the thicker section enters the bore, it starts to pick up fouling and push it out in front. The bronze bristles loosen any stubborn fouling which is then removed as the thickest part of the 'snake' enters the bore. After several passes your gun or rifle is squeaky clean.

One of the greatest advantages of a Boresnake is that it can be carried in your pocket; this has revolutionised field cleaning. Perhaps the only disadvantage is that you will need several of them if you own rifles and shotguns with a wide divergence of bore size; they are not cheap. At least with a rod, all you have to buy is different sizes of brushes and jags.

Flexible cables

There are some cleaning kits which use plastic-coated steel cable to make a flexible, semi-rigid cleaning tool. The brush or jag screws onto one end while the other terminates in a T-bar handle. The cable is passed down the barrel. The requisite attachment is fitted and then pulled back to clean the bore. These are quite time-consuming but have a place where space is limited. For instance, they take up little room in a day sack and are useful for field cleaning.

You will also see some multi-gun cleaning kits which have shotgun and rifle rods, plus a wide variety of brushes, jags and mops, all put up in a single case. This is a good idea in principle but really look at the quality of the rods before buying. The test has to be: how will this rod stand up to hard use? If it is bendy and flimsy, it is likely to snap at the joint. In my opinion, a one-piece rod is always the best option for a rifle.

Dealing with obstructions

It is inevitable that you will touch the ground with your rifle or shotgun barrel from time to time. When this happens, all too often you get a plug of mud or compacted snow in the muzzle. NEVER TRY TO REMOVE THIS BY A FIRING ANOTHER CARTRIDGE. If you do it with a shotgun, you will blow the end three inches off your barrels. Not only will your gun be ruined but those around you will be endangered by flying razor sharp fragments. If you fire a cartridge in a rifle with a blocked barrel then the likelihood is that the barrel will bulge and accuracy will be seriously compromised.

If you carry a cleaning rod in the boot of your car you can deal with any blockage easily. If the blockage is snow, warming the barrel with your breath and hands will sometimes loosen it enough for you to prise it out with a suitable instrument. I got a plug of snow in my tubes last season and by carefully pushing the little saw on my Swiss Army knife through it, I was able to hook it out.

After you have removed the blockage, make sure that you can see the sky through the tube before loading a cartridge.

In similar vein, I always carry a shotgun cartridge extractor in case I get a case stuck in the chamber. Mine is an antique pincer type that will deal with cases from 12 bore to .410 and smaller. You can also get ring types for specific gauges. Some Continental folding hunting knives incorporate a cartridge extractor in their guards. These are very useful companions, especially if they have a corkscrew on them too.

Damage caused to the muzzles by firing when they were blocked by mud

CLEANING SHOTGUNS

Confirm that the gun is unloaded; dismantle it into barrels, stock/action and forend, then lay the parts out on your newspaper or cleaning mat.

Then take another sheet of newspaper and crumple part of it into a ball that will pass easily through the barrels. Printers' ink is slightly greasy and this seems to provide lubrication as the paper ball passes up the bore. The purpose is to push all of the loose fouling out of the bores. Some powders leave more combustion residue than others; put simply, they have a dirtier burn and leave flakes of soot behind. These will be pushed out by the wadded paper. The easiest way to do this is to push the paper ball into the chamber, follow it with the rod or a length of dowel, place the rod/dowel end on the floor and gently drop the barrels onto it. You should hear a squeaking sound as the paper is progressively pushed up the bores. This method utilises the barrel's weight to push the paper through. It also minimises the risk of breaking the rod by heavy-handedness.

Next, soak a phosphor bronze brush with bore solvent and scrub the barrels with it. The aim here is to remove any plastic deposits and leading. If these are not deeply ingrained, a couple of passes of the brush on its own will shift them. Plastic deposits show up as a grey smear in the bore. When the solvent starts to loosen them they look like grey slime. I remain to be convinced that deposits really affect the gun's pattern adversely. There is one way to prevent them occurring and that is to use fibre wads only. I find it hard to reconcile that, while I recycle my empty plastic cases for environmental reasons, I continue to deposit large quantities of plastic around the countryside. That does not stack up somehow.

Push another ball of newspaper through the bores to dry up the solvent and remove anything which it has dislodged. Then, take a patch of the correct size and run that up the bores. If you have done your stuff, it should come out with little or no fouling on it. Repeat until the patch comes out clean.

Run a cocktail stick along the joint between the ribs and the barrels. This will dislodge any accumulated dirt which can then be brushed off. If you have a ventilated top rib, use the cocktail stick to pick out dirt from the spaces. Pay particular attention to the extractors and clean under them with a rag. If they can be removed easily, do so and give them a thorough wipe before you reassemble them.

If your gun has variable chokes, take them out and swill in petrol. Run a cloth around the threads in the barrel to remove any grit or dirt. Wipe the choke with either a little graphite grease or petroleum jelly and make sure that it is really screwed home properly. If it is not, then the phenomenon of 'choke pick up' can occur. When a choke is not properly screwed home, every time the gun is fired some of the lead pellets hit the gap between barrel wall and choke tube. Eventually, some pellets get lodged in it. This causes the choke tube to distort until it eventually leaves the gun's muzzle with a subsequent shot charge. This not only ruins the gun but also creates a hazard to people like beaters or flags in front. The only remedy is to have the barrels shortened,

Choke tubes in petrol with cleaning brush

with the damaged portion being amputated.

Lastly, run a wool mop covered in a little oil through the bores. Do not drench the barrels. What you are trying to achieve is to make an impermeable barrier between the atmosphere and the steel. Too much oil attracts dust and other minor debris. The exterior of the barrels should be wiped with an oily rag. In my opinion, a better alternative is to wipe them with a silicone cloth or coat them with a hard wax polish. Both are very water repellent and because they leave a hard and shiny surface, they do not attract dust.

Put the barrels to one side and take up the stock and action. Wipe the stock with a damp piece of kitchen paper. This will remove any dried mud. Chequered areas, such as the wrist and butt-plate, should be brushed with a toothbrush. Wipe the metal with an oily rag or silicone cloth. On a side-by-side, give the well that engages the lump a good picking out with a cocktail stick or

stiff-bristled artist's brush. On an over-and-under gun, make sure the trunnions are carefully wiped to prevent the build-up of dirt or grit.

If your gun has disc-set strikers make sure that the discs have not shaken loose, otherwise the gun will not close properly. An easy way to do this is to lay a steel ruler on its edge over them. If they are starting to work loose, this will show by the ruler not lying flush with the action. Unless you have a striker wrench, they will have to be tightened by a gunsmith.

Make sure the cocking arms move freely. Lubricate any moving parts with a drop of oil on the tip of a cocktail stick. Again, do not use too much. If you have a gun with hand-detachable locks, remove them from time to time, give them a brush, lightly oil them and re-install.

Give the chequered areas on the forend a brush. Wipe the forend iron with an oily rag and lightly oil any bearing surfaces. Lastly, make sure that all screws are tightened and that they have not worked loose. Put the gun back together again and lock it in your gun cabinet.

Self-loading shotgun dismantled for cleaning

This procedure applies to any shotgun, but if you use a self-loader or pump-action, there are a few additions. Always remove the barrel before cleaning. Sometimes, a cartridge will lurk in the tubular magazine. If the barrel is not on the gun there is no chance it can ever reach the chamber. Remove the bolt and wipe off any fouling. Brush out the interior of the frame. Oil the bolt lightly, making sure that the firing pin is lubricated so that it runs back and forth easily. Reassemble and dry-fire the gun, pointing it in a safe direction. Store with the action closed and the springs at rest. Make sure you reassemble a self-loader correctly; if in doubt look for a manual on the internet or try YouTube.

If you have a gas-operated self-loading shotgun (most are) you will need to make sure that the gas ports do not get blocked by carbon build-up. When a gas-operated gun fires, part of the gas is tapped off through a minute port(s) under the barrel. This bears on a piston attached to the bolt. Gas pressure pushes the piston back against the pressure of the recoil spring which is normally housed in a tube at the back of the action recessed in a hole in the stock. When the bolt reaches the end of its travel, the empty case is ejected. The bolt then runs forward under the force of the recoil spring, picks up a new cartridge from the lifter and rams it into the chamber ready for firing.

As the gas runs through the ports, carbon fouling can build up and prevent self-loading operation. It is important to keep the gas system clean. Use plenty of bore solvent which will dissolve the fouling. Once it builds up, it is difficult to shift. A small twist drill (approx 2mm) will help remove really stubborn carbon fouling in the ports.

If you are a regular user of a hammer gun, you may need to remove the strikers to prevent them binding in the action. A stuck striker may cause a cartridge to detonate as the gun closes. The easiest way to remove the strikers is with a crank-handled striker wrench. I don't think any gun equipment supplier offers one these days, but they sometimes turn up in auctions or as dealer's stock. It is possible to adapt a very small spanner or a model-maker's socket wrench.

CLEANING SPORTING RIFLES

Wiping a field-stripped rifle action after cleaning the bore.

Rimfire

Strangely enough, .22 rimfire rifles with lead bullets do not need much cleaning and tend to shoot more consistently when they are not cleaned regularly. In fact, some target rifle shooters rarely clean their rifles and assert that if they do, they have to be shot in again with several boxes of ammunition. That is for precision target shooting; with hunting rifles it is not nearly so critical.

.22RF cartridges have externally lubricated bullets and, if nothing else, that lubrication which has accumulated on the bolt face and in the action needs removing. A combination of a stiff brush and cocktail sticks will get rid of it.

Remove the bolt and otherwise field strip the rifle for cleaning. If you decide to clean the bore, use a proper sized bristle or nylon – not phosphor bronze – brush fitted to a rod whose diameter is as close to the bore size as possible. These small bore rods are very whippy and if used vigorously, they might bend and damage the rifling. The best type of rod is a one-piece plastic-coated stainless steel one. Avoid jointed rods as they are not as strong and grit can build up in the joint areas and get transferred to the bore.

The brush will loosen dirt, lubricant and lead fouling. For the first few strokes, push the rod through until the brush emerges, unscrew it and pull the rod back. This avoids any muck adhering to the brush being dragged back into the bore. The brush can be followed by a cleaning patch soaked in bore solvent carried in a loop attachment. That will get rid of the rest of the fouling. There is no need to oil the bore excessively, a quick wipe with just a drop of oil on a mop is enough. .22 rimfire rifles only need occasional cleaning. The outside of the rifle can be given a wipe with an oily rag, taking care to not to get any oil on the lenses of the optics.

Realistically, a quick pull through with a boresnake once in a while will be enough to keep a rimfire rifle in shooting order.

Centre-fire and rimfires using copper-jacketed bullets

Metal-jacketed bullets from centre-fire rifles can leave a lot of metallic fouling (mainly copper or nickel) in the bore which, if not removed, can lead to a reduction in accuracy. The main objective when cleaning a centre-fire rifle is to remove that metallic fouling and to prevent it building up in the first place. To that end a quick pull through with a boresnake is normally adequate after a few shots. After a long session on the range then the full regime needs applying. The products of combustion are generally easy to remove; metallic fouling less so.

Put a phosphor bronze brush on the rod and make sure it is well soaked in solvent. Pass it through the bore a few times from the chamber end, unscrewing it as it emerges at the muzzle. Always use a rod guide to make sure it goes in centrally. Allow the solvent to work for a few minutes and then wrap a proper-sized patch around the jag. Push it through the bore until it emerges and remove it. The first few patches will come out black as they remove the combustion fouling. Eventually, the deposit on them will turn blue as they start to remove the metallic fouling. Use plenty of solvent and always allow it sufficient time to do its work before passing another patch through.

When the patch comes out clean, you can oil the bore with a drop of oil on a wool mop. Remember, the bore will have to be cleaned of the oil before firing. Firing a cartridge in an oily barrel will produce some aberrant results on the target and may generate dangerous pressures. Rifle barrels must always be wiped before firing. This is particularly important with a hunting rifle. What would be a good shot from a dry barrel may cause the bullet to go elsewhere than the point of aim and wound the animal. As ethical hunters we cannot allow that to happen. The amount of oil you apply will depend on the frequency of use. A rifle that is going into storage for three months needs a good coating; one that is going out next week may not need oiling at all.

Give the bolt a good clean and pick any muck out of its crevices with a cocktail stick. Pay particular attention to the striker hole. It is a good idea to learn how to take a bolt to pieces and give it a thorough clean occasionally. If you haven't got the manual, there is probably one online. Failing that, look for a YouTube video tutorial.

Wipe the stock with a damp cloth. If walnut, a little boiled linseed will maintain its natural glow. If synthetic, then a little car dashboard polish will make it look very good indeed. Wipe the metal with an oily rag and you are done.

CLEANING AIR RIFLES

As air rifles do not use the gases of chemical combustion to propel their missiles, they do not get as dirty as conventional firearms. Nevertheless, they do get dirty and need occasional cleaning. Perhaps a useful indicator that cleaning is probably needed is when you have finished a tin of pellets.

Pre-charged pneumatic (PCP) air rifles with magazines proliferate these days; before attempting to clean one you must remove both the magazine and the air reservoir. By doing this you remove any risk of a pellet being fed into the breech and propelled out by a charge of compressed air. There is one sure-fire method of checking that a PCP is empty and that is to load and fire a single pellet from it into a safe backstop such as an old telephone directory. The moderator needs taking off as this makes the bore much more accessible for cleaning.

There is no need to cock a springer completely as most will open sufficiently for you to see through the barrel. Carbon dioxide bulbs need to be removed before cleaning, too. This can be done only when they are completely empty. It is common sense to keep any container of compressed gas away from heat sources.

Push a rod of the correct diameter into the muzzle to dislodge any pellet that may have lodged in the bore. Keep the air rifle pointing away from you while doing this. Once you are satisfied that there is neither air nor projectile in the rifle, screw a bristle brush on your cleaning rod and gently brush the bore. You will have to do this from the muzzle end, so it is essential to use a rod guide to protect the crown. As you are not trying to remove the products of combustion, you do not need to scrub vigorously. Most of the dirt in the bore will have dropped in when the air rifle was being used. All you are trying to do is push it out again. The rest tends to be tiny bits of metal scraped off the pellet when it runs up the barrel. As a rule of thumb, the cheaper the air rifle, the rougher the bore and the more likely it will be to accumulate lead. It's a good idea to put a piece of tape sticky-side-up at the back of the loading port. This will catch any debris that the brush dislodges.

After using the brush you can run a thin cloth patch through the bore just to remove any dirt adhering to the bottom of the lands. I always avoid getting mineral oil in the barrel and action of a PCP as it might damage the O ring seals. Some form of silicone-based lubricant is preferable.

The individual pellet holes in the magazine need a brush passing through them from time to time. Using a cocktail stick, put a tiny drop of oil on the bolt so that it runs back and forward smoothly.

There is a very good plastic-coated cable pull-through on the market specially designed for cleaning PCPs. It takes account of the fact that the loading port of a PCP is small and difficult to get at. The cable has a thin loop at one end. It is pushed down the bore until the loop appears in the port. This is then loaded with a couple of cloth patches and the cable pulled out with one fluid movement. The process is repeated until the outer patch is clean.

Another very good cleaning method for air rifles is to fire a purpose-built felt pellet through the bore. There are several brands of these and they are all very good for a quick and easy clean. As the felt runs up the bore, it pushes all the dirt in front of it.

If you have a springer air rifle it is easier to clean, as you can see through the bore. The barrel can be cleaned from the breech end. A word of warning: beware of using too much oil in any air rifle as it may cause the phenomenon called dieseling. This occurs when oil vapour gets mixed with air and which is then ignited by the heat generated as it is compressed by the piston running forward. This combustion not only damages the air rifle's interior but, worst of all, may take it over the 12 ft lb limit in the Firearms (Dangerous Air Weapons) Rules, 1969. Exceeding this limit is a strict liability criminal offence. Go easy on the oil and you will not be troubled by it. It is worth investing in a small chronoscope (about £50 or so) so that you can check on the kinetic energy level without having to take the rifle to a shop. Most air rifles are set perilously close to the 12 ft lb limit and dieseling or even injudicious fiddling can easily take it over. It is standard police procedure to test any air rifle that might be seized and it is surprising how many are over the limit. Buy a chronoscope and make sure yours is not one of them.

When you have cleaned the bore, the stock can be wiped with a damp cloth and the metal parts protected with an oily rag. Avoid getting oil on the lenses of the telescope or other optics. Give the threads of the moderator a dab of petroleum jelly or graphite grease. That will ensure that it unscrews easily next time you remove it.

Remember if you have youngsters under 18 in your house, you must take reasonable precautions to prevent them gaining unauthorised access to your air weapons (Crime and Security Act, 2010). This does not mean airguns have to be locked in a steel cabinet; a locked cupboard will do. This may seem a chore but don't forget that an air rifle is more than capable of killing someone, especially a child. In my experience, cable and trigger locks are a waste of time and don't actually allow you to discharge your statutory duty, as most air rifle trigger guards are only secured by two screws.

The UK law still allows 14–17 year olds to shoot unsupervised on private premises where they have permission to be.

CLEANING EX-MILITARY RIFLES

6.5m Japanese Type 44 cavalry carbine

Although the basics for cleaning a military surplus rifle is the same as a sporting rifle, there are some aspects that need special techniques. It's important to realise that many military surplus rifles are old, dating back to at least the Second World War. It is likely that they will have suffered neglect at the hands of their former owners. It is also likely that they have lain in some dusty warehouse or grubby arsenal before the government that owned them decided to turn them into hard cash. All things considered, they need a good looking-over before use. In jurisdictions with a gun barrel proof regime, you know that at least your piece of military history is safe to use. In jurisdictions with no proof laws, such as the US, I recommend a thorough inspection by a competent gunsmith. Ask him to fire a few rounds out of the rifle remotely just to be certain that it is not going to blow when you press the trigger on the range.

It is likely that the importer and then the retailer will have done some basic cleaning in order to make the rifles more saleable. Shooters are more inclined to buy if they see the words 'good bore' in an advert. However, that cleaning will be just enough to make the rifle fit to sit on a dealer's gun rack.

Many rifles are preserved in Cosmoline, which is a thick petroleum-based liquid wax. It is poured over and into the action while warm. In short, it gets everywhere. Whilst Cosmoline is very good preservative, it is very hard to shift; the only really effective way to get rid of it is to scrape or wipe off as much as possible and then wipe the major parts with a petroleum soaked rag. Smaller parts can be steeped in a petrol bath until all the goo has dissolved. It will also get into the wood fibres so the techniques that I describe for dealing with an oil-soaked stock in the Antiques section will need to be used here.

It is always a good idea to completely dismantle a Cosmoline-covered rifle. If you don't, you will find it oozing grease when it heats up after a few cartridges. I owned a 7.92mm Portuguese M1904/39 Mauser-Verguiero rifle that looked clean when I bought it. However, after I had wound a couple of clips of cartridges through it, Cosmoline began to ooze out of every orifice. I had to take it down to the smallest part and get rid of the filthy stuff.

It is very important to wipe the bore before the first firing otherwise the accuracy will suffer and you may find that it may cause excessive pressures. The famous US ballistician General Julian Hatcher actually describes .30-06 M1903 Springfield rifle actions failing because someone had not checked that the bore was clear of Cosmoline before firing. A bullet from the powerful .30-06 cartridge fired into thick unyielding grease was more than even this robust action could stand.

Wipe the bore thoroughly with a patch soaked in petrol. Do so until it comes out without any traces of oil on it. You can then get to work with a phosphor bronze brush, either soaked in soluble oil and water mix or a powerful proprietary bore solvent. Sometimes old military rifle barrels just will not come clean and, providing that the rifle shoots straight, then there is not much more that you can do. Do not expect target accuracy from old military rifles. They were designed to hit a man-sized target at about 300 metres.

In extremis, I have used a rod tipped with a wire brush in an electric drill. This is run back and forth at a relatively low speed until the rust and fouling is loosened. A jag wrapped in coarse wire wool is equally as effective. The British Army Lee Enfield pull-through had a loop for a piece of steel gauze for really dirty or rusty barrels. However, this was always a thing of last resort and had to be authorised by an officer. The drill or wire brush techniques are not something I use every day. They are reserved for especially dirty barrels.

The last resort. Bronze brush and electric drill

I have a .303 Short Magazine Lee Enfield rifle that I bought in the 1980s. Its bore was filthy and despite my best efforts over more than three decades, remains so. For all that, I can still put all 10 shots into a Figure 11 target at 200m with it. I think you have to be pragmatic and accept the accumulated dirt plus soldierly neglect will never be totally removed. If it shoots straight then don't agonise too much that the bore isn't shiny.

Some ex-military ammunition – especially Soviet – has mercuric primers that are very corrosive. Any rifle that has fired this ammunition will need a good swabbing with a patch soaked in household ammonia. This neutralises the corrosive effect. In fact the Soviets used to issue what they described as an 'alkaline solvent' to complement the oil in their cleaning kits.

Military ammunition often has a coloured varnish around its primers. This has two functions; it gives a water proof seal and also helps to distinguish the nature of the ammunition. Small bits break loose on firing and can clog up the firing pin hole. It is always a good idea to dismantle a rifle bolt completely and give it a really good clean after every 100 shots.

Some bolts are easier to dismantle than others. The easiest is the Japanese Arisaka bolt which comes to bits with just a twist of the safety knob. Lee Enfield bolt heads unscrew. The Mosin Nagant, Lebel and Mauser 88 bolts all have separate heads which are easily removed to get at the striker. The Mauser 98 bolt is a little more complicated to take to bits. First, set the 'flag' safety to its central position. Next push in the little stud on the bolt collar and you will find that you can unscrew the body. You are then left with the collar attached to the striker by the cocking piece. Push the striker into a small hole in a bit of wood and press down until the cocking piece is clear of the collar. Turn the cocking piece a quarter turn in any direction and it comes off

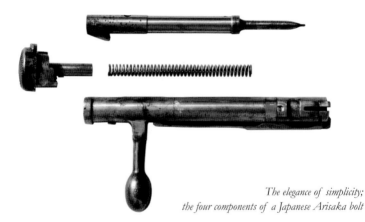

The elegance of simplicity;
the four components of a Japanese Arisaka bolt

the striker. That whole assembly can then be taken to bits. After about 1916, many military Mausers had a dismounting boss permanently fitted to their buttstocks. This makes bolt disassembly easy.

Pay particular attention to the tip of the striker and make sure it is wiped clean. The striker hole can be cleaned out with a cocktail stick. A screwdriver with a patch wrapped around the blade is very good for cleaning inside the bolt body. I always dismantle magazines, as they attract dirt and will jam if it builds up.

If you have a military rifle with a bayonet and you are going to fire it with the bayonet fixed, protect the part of the blade nearest the muzzle with broad sticky tape or sticky-backed plastic. This is especially important if using black powder. The muzzle flash can really pit a blade if left uncleaned.

In the event that you have a falling-block rifle that cannot be cleaned from the breech end, you have no choice but to clean it from the muzzle. Always use a bore guide to protect the crown. That part of a rifle barrel can really affect accuracy if it becomes damaged.

If you can't work out how to strip a rifle or its bolt, you will find the answer on YouTube. There are thousands of instructional videos made by people who have had to learn the hard way. I use it regularly.

Shooting a classic military rifle is like shaking hands with history; you can read any number of books where armchair ballisticians speculate on its effectiveness. Having actually fired one, you will be able to speak from experience rather than accepting their received knowledge at face value.

CLEANING BLACK POWDER FIREARMS

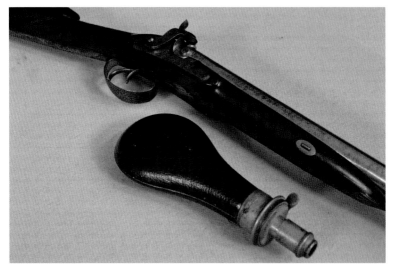

Introduction

Black powder (gunpowder) is a mechanical mixture of potassium nitrate, sulphur and carbon in varying proportions. When ignited it burns very rapidly, producing a large cloud of white smoke, combustion gases and a sticky residue. Gunpowder is not an efficient propellant as only about 60% of it is turned into gas on ignition. The remaining 40% is solid material resulting from the combustion. It takes the form of a sooty black deposit that coats the surface of any part of the firearm exposed to the combustion. It is very hygroscopic (moisture absorbent) and, as it contains sulphur, it becomes an acidic corrosive which causes rust and pitting to the steel if not neutralised and removed soon after firing.

Black powder residue builds up during firing, making the firearm more difficult to load after every shot. It can also get into the mechanism of a firearm, causing it to malfunction. It causes corrosion and ultimately pitting, which may threaten the integrity of the firearm if allowed to develop unchecked. Accordingly, prompt cleaning is essential after a muzzle-loading firearm has been used.

How soon you need to clean a black powder gun before corrosion damage takes place will depend on the amount of moisture in the atmosphere. I have fired a revolver on a hot, sunny day and corrosion had not occurred some eight hours later. Equally, I have shot grouse in Scotland with a muzzle-loading shotgun in a rainy environment and corrosion had occurred before we had returned to our quarters. The corrosion process may be slowed down by the application of water-displacing spray, e.g. WD40, which forms a temporary barrier between the residue and the metal. However, proper cleaning should be undertaken as soon as practicable. If you do not clean any black powder firearm promptly, the likely result is corrosion and damage.

There are several black powder substitutes available of which Pyrodex is the most commonly encountered. It is not classified in law as an explosive so no explosives certificate is needed to possess it. Although it does not work in the priming pan of a flintlock, it ignites very well in a percussion gun and is excellent when loaded in cartridges. The downside is that the fouling it leaves behind seems much more prone to forming rust than ordinary gunpowder. Consequently, great care needs to be exercised when cleaning a firearm in which it has been used and extreme vigilance exercised thereafter. If you detect any hint of rust, clean the gun again.

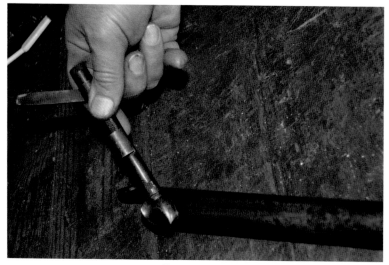

Removing a percussion nipple with a proper nipple wrench

Muzzle-loading long arms

It is always preferable to remove the barrel from the stock. First, check that the firearm is unloaded by dropping the rammer down the barrel. If you hear a metallic clang, then it is safe to proceed. A dull thud or an over-projecting rammer means that there is a load in the barrel that must be removed first.

For a percussion firearm, remove the nipples with the nipple wrench. Half-fill a bucket with warm water and add a squirt of washing-up liquid. Wrap a piece of rag around a jag on a suitable rod. This does not need to be very tight as it will act as a plunger which draws in and expels water from the barrel. Put the barrel breech-end in the water and insert the rod into it. As it gets wet the, the rag swells and acts as a piston. Working the rod back and forth will force water through the nipple hole/vent. This loosens fouling and the sudden rush will really flush out the chamber(s). Do that for several strokes and then discard the dirty water. Put a funnel in the muzzle and pour a kettle-full of boiling water down it. Be careful, the barrel gets very hot and you will need a thick glove. The boiling water helps dissolve and flush out any fouling. The heat also helps the barrel to dry. Wipe out with a piece of rag on the jag soaked in bore solvent to remove any stubborn fouling. Rifle barrels also benefit from scrubbing with a brush to remove fouling from the grooves.

Run some clean rag down the bore to help dry the barrel and either dry with a hair dryer or find somewhere with gentle heat for the barrel to dry. When thoroughly dry, oil the bore with a mop and give the exterior a rub over with an oily rag.

Steep the nipple in some black powder solvent and make sure the flash hole is clear. Then clean, dry and grease the threads before reinstalling.

Remove the lock from the stock and clean thoroughly by wiping with solvent. For flintlocks, always remove the flint from the cock. This is for safety reasons as the flint is surgically sharp and the cock is attached to a powerful spring. You do not want your fingers in its way if the sear trips accidentally while cleaning. Some flintlocks have detachable priming pans: always remove them for cleaning.

When cleaning a percussion lock, always pay particular attention to the hammer nose and remove fouling from the caps.

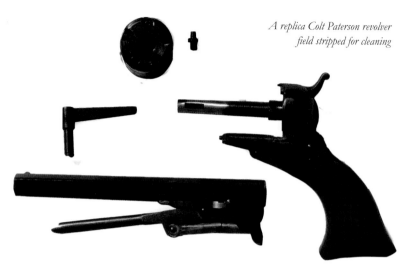

*A replica Colt Paterson revolver
field stripped for cleaning*

Revolvers

Cleaning a black powder revolver is a messy and laborious affair. Large quantities of hot water plus a proprietary solvent are needed, along with specialist implements and rag or kitchen paper.

My recommended procedure is as follows:

- Dismantle the revolver, removing its cylinder from the frame.
- Unscrew the percussion cap nipples using a specialist wrench.
- Put the cylinder and nipples in a basin of hot soapy water to remove the worst of the fouling.
- Push some rag through the barrel bore to dislodge the worst of the fouling.
- Using a small funnel, pour boiling water down the breech and pass the rag through again.

Where revolvers, such as Colts, have detachable barrels, they can be put into the water along with the cylinders. It is always good practice to remove the wooden grips to give access to the lock mechanism and to remove any fouling or percussion cap fragments that have become lodged in it. This also prevents any water damage to the wood.

Lightly brush out the lock mechanism with a stiff-bristled artist's brush. Don't be afraid to dismantle mechanisms, as they are generally simple, mass-produced designs. This allows for very thorough cleaning which may be necessary if a large number of shots have been fired, e.g. after a club night. Black powder fouling can spread widely throughout a mechanism, carrying corrosion with it. As you disassemble the mechanism, keep the components together in a single container – a magnetic tray is ideal. Make a note of the order in which you removed them; reverse this when re-assembling. It is a good idea to stick small screws to a piece of card with adhesive tape and number them. This not only protects against loss but also ensures they go back in the right order.

When the worst of the fouling has been removed, clean the individual components again using the powder solvent to remove all traces of it and neutralise any acidity. Thoroughly dry the components, preferably using a gentle heat source such as a hair dryer or the plate rack on a cooker. When the parts are warm and dry, lightly oil them and reassemble the revolver. It can then be placed in secure storage but should be inspected 24 hours later to ensure that no corrosion is present due to condensation etc. Steel cabinets are notorious for producing condensation on their surfaces and contents, especially in cold, damp weather.

Give the wooden grips a thorough wipe clean with a damp rag. If they have been oil-finished, rub some boiled linseed oil into them periodically. Make sure they are completely dry before re-installing them.

To clean a black powder revolver thoroughly takes about an hour. The process requires a sink with a draining board as well as a kettle to provide boiling water. In my experience, stainless steel sinks are preferable, as ceramic ones can be damaged if a heavy metallic part such as a cylinder is dropped into them; equally, the part itself may sustain damage.

Brass cartridge cases

If you have a black powder breech-loader, its cartridge cases will need careful cleaning too. Doing each case individually is a real chore, so try this. Decap the cases and place them mouth uppermost in a glass jar. Cover with boiling water and add some stain remover powder, like Vanish or OxiClean. The cases start to foam immediately and much of the fouling ends up floating on the top of that foam. Leave for 30 minutes and then pour away the solution. Rinse with more boiling water and dry with a hair dryer or place on a radiator overnight. A low oven is an effective heat source too. When dry, clean them for 30 minutes in a tumbling machine and they will look like new. Another solution, that works without the need for a tumbler, is made from 4 parts boiling water, 1 part spirit vinegar, a tablespoon of salt and a good squirt of washing-up liquid. Leave the cases in this for 30 minutes, rinse and dry thoroughly.

Post-cleaning vigilance is very important for black powder guns – more so than for smokeless. Watch for any rust and tackle it immediately if it appears.

RCBS vibratory cartridge case cleaning

RESTORING ANTIQUE AND VINTAGE GUNS

At some time, most of us get the urge to buy an antique or vintage shotgun that needs a little work. Restoring any firearm is a very satisfying thing. Not only do you give a piece of sporting history its dignity back, you also provide yourself with a rare opportunity to experience the way our forebears shot, if you then go on to use it. Restoring an antique or vintage gun for use is much like having an old car: it will not be something you go to work in everyday, but it's nice for a trip out on a Sunday. The same holds true for a hammer gun or a muzzle-loader. Taking it out on the Boxing Day shoot just adds to that occasion.

As a general rule, if you are uncertain about doing something, don't do it. Practise on something that does not matter. My uncle Herbert had a scrap shotgun on his farm. It provided me with much useful practice in dismantling guns. Lastly, always be certain that what you are going to do will tone in with what the gun probably looked like originally. For example, chrome plating a hammer gun may give good protection but it will look truly ghastly.

The first step in restoring an old gun is to take it to bits. How far you go will depend on your skill and confidence. These days you are likely to have a mobile phone with a decent camera; photograph every stage so that you know which part goes where when you come to reassemble it. It is important not to lose anything, so I get a cardboard box big enough to act as a tray to keep everything together. Components from the major groups are best put straight into re-sealable freezer bags as they are dismantled. I also try to take a gun to pieces in an environment where, if a small part is dropped, it can be easily retrieved. The clutter and dirty floor of a workshop is not the place to take a gunlock to pieces. I also use a tray with 25mm high edges to stop small parts from falling somewhere inaccessible. That, combined with a smaller magnetic tray, reduces the risk of mishaps dramatically. Magnetic trays are cheap and can be bought online and from tool stalls at game fairs. They are a good investment. Another tool that I find invaluable is a magnet on an extending wand like a car radio aerial. Armed with that, even the smallest screw that has rolled into a corner can be easily retrieved.

Make sure you have the proper tools for the job. Many guns are disfigured or damaged by someone who is too lazy or mean to obtain the proper tools. Damaging something you set out to improve is a retrograde step that normally has to be put right by a professional. Don't go there. It is vital to use a proper set of turn-screws otherwise the screw heads will be damaged when you try to get them out. If you come across a gun where some vandal has damaged screw slots, they can be improved by gently hammering them (peening) to push the metal back and then tidying them up with a Swiss file. If you really can't live with them afterwards, get the screw heads re-formed by someone with a MIG welder and re cut the slots. The screws will have to be toned in with rest of the gun if you do that (see below).

Some screws are very difficult to remove. The careful application of a little releasing fluid will often break the bond that is preventing them from coming out. Give a stubborn screw a spray and leave for 30 mins to allow the fluid to penetrate. Then clamp the component containing the screw in the vice and, gripping the handle of your turnscrew with both hands and pushing against the screw with your body weight, try to see if it will budge. It is always a good idea to clean any muck out of the screw slot with a cocktail stick to allow the turnscrew blade to get in as deeply as possible. A useful technique once you feel it move is to turn it back and forth a little; that tends to loosen it. It goes without saying that you need to put some thick padding in the vice jaws otherwise they will mark the thing it is holding. Old carpet scraps glued to scrap wood are ideal. I have seen an ingenious self-closing set used by craftsmen in the Birmingham gun trade. These were no more than the padded strips joined by pieces of springy steel at the bottom. If you are going to be doing a lot of restoration, these self-closers save a lot of time. Magnetic jaws with rubber inserts are good too. These are inexpensive and should be replaced as they become worn or damaged.

When taking the screws out of a lockplate, I find it useful to screw them into a piece of card with a diagram of the plate to ensure that you know the hole from which they came. It also serves to stop them getting lost. That is not a major issue with a machine-made gun; with one that is hand-made there may be a minute dimensional difference that makes screw A a tight fit if is screwed back into screw C's hole.

The threads and slots of removed screws should be brushed with a wire brush and washed in petrol to remove any

Dismantled lock screws pushed into card to ensure correct placement for re-assembly

dirt. The same applies for any other small metal components.

It is essential to use a mainspring vice to remove a mainspring. Pliers or Mole grips are just not suitable. Cock the lock and slip the jaws of the vice over it, making sure that the longest jaw extends over the majority of the longest limb of the spring. Tighten the vice with its thumbscrew. When it will tighten up no more, trip the trigger sear and let the hammer fall under control. The spring will stay compressed. It and the vice can be easily lifted clear. Leave the spring in the vice and clean in situ.

An alternative to stripping a lock is to soak it for 72 hours in home-made releasing fluid (brake fluid and acetone). This gets rid of the grime and any gummy oil deposits without the need to dismantle it. The dirt will normally come off with a stiff bristle brush. Wear surgical gloves when using solvents and throw the old fluid away (be responsible about this) and rinse with some new.

Rust and accumulated grime will normally come off if rubbed with some 0000 steel wool soaked in meths. Change the wool often: rust is hard and very abrasive. The wool is hard enough to remove any dirt and soft enough not to scratch any finish or age patina.

If you have made a new part or really cleaned up an existing one, it may need toning so it does not look out of place with the rest of the gun. Use gun barrel browning solution to do this. Heat the part with a blow torch until it is too hot to touch; apply a little of the solution with a swab made from a piece of cotton cloth on a bit of dowel. It should hiss and go brown. Leave it somewhere damp for a few days and it should be red with rust. Brush with a brass wire brush and repeat the process until the desired shade is reached. Before waxing, the acidity needs to be neutralised. I put the finished piece in a solution of bicarbonate of soda for an hour.

Nipples often get rusted in, as percussion cap residues were very corrosive. In fact, many nipples were fixed with a thin copper washer between them and the barrel breech to prevent any corrosive bridge forming. Releasing fluid applied from both ends is essential before trying to remove them with a key. Make sure that the key is a tight fit otherwise the nipple flats will get damaged. Put the cylinder or barrels in the vice before trying to remove the nipples. A little heat may be needed to shift a really stubborn one. Use one of those little jeweller's torches or a turbo-lighter with an angled spout and keep the flame localised. Make sure that there is not an old charge lurking in the breech otherwise you will get a nasty surprise, as heat and gunpowder do not mix. If a broken nipple cannot be unscrewed then it will have to be drilled out. Run progressively larger drills into the hole until the remaining metal collapses and comes out. The threads may need to be refreshed with the proper size engineer's tap. If that does not work then your only option is a light engineering firm with spark erosion equipment.

Any brass furniture – normally found on military guns – can be soaked in spirit vinegar. Any corrosion will disappear after a few hours and the brass can be rubbed to a pleasing sheen with a soft cloth. I hate, loathe and detest brass polishes. They fill crevices with horrid powder residue and are very abrasive. They make brass look like it was won at yesterday's funfair. It needs to be clean but with a subtle age patina.

Stocks benefit from being cleaned with meths or acetone applied with rags. They will remove a lot of dirt. Change the cloths often and do not leave indoors overnight as they can spontaneously combust. If the stock is really dirty, soak some 0000 wire wool in meths and rub gently. Wipe regularly with a cloth soaked in meths. When the stock is clean, it may need some colour putting back. Traditionally, stocks were dyed with root of alkanet, but I find that proprietary spirt based dyes give good colours. Suede dye is very good too. There are some proprietary stock dyes available, some of which combine colour with finish so that a stock can be coloured and finished in one go.

Sometimes it may be necessary to remove barrel pins and those which secure furniture. This needs to be done with a punch that is slightly smaller in diameter to the pin itself. Make sure that it is really on the pin before tapping it, otherwise you will drive it into the stock.

Chequering can be cleaned with a toothbrush. Preparatory work by running a cocktail stick in the grooves will loosen any dirt. Use meths or acetone, gently brushing it in the direction of the longest strokes to dislodge the dirt. When that is done, the crosswise strokes can be cleaned. It is surprising how easily chequering gets clogged with dirt, oil and old varnish. Often once thoroughly cleaned, it regains its sharpness.

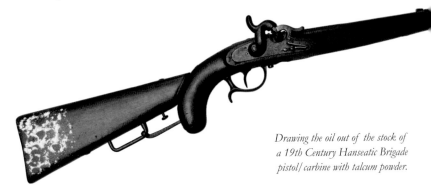

Drawing the oil out of the stock of a 19th Century Hanseatic Brigade pistol/carbine with talcum powder.

Sometimes a stock will be soaked with oil. That is bad news as mineral oil destroys wood fibres. The best way of removing a lot of the oil is to lay the stock on newspaper in a sunny window. After a while the heat of the sun will start to sweat the oil out of the wood. Wipe off the excess and then dust the stock with fuller's earth or talcum powder. This is very absorbent and will take up more of the oil. The oily paste can be easily wiped off. Do this until very little oil continues to be exuded. Wipe down with meths or acetone. Sometimes you will find that a stock is too soft to allow a wood screw to bite. The best remedy for this is to drill the screw hole out and glue a suitable piece of dowel into it. When the glue is dry, drill a small pilot hole and the screw should go in and really bite.

In this age of wonderful modern glues, it is easy to glue up a crack or stick back a splinter. When dealing with a crack, try to force it open a little so that plenty of glue can be introduced. It needs to be clamped close for best results. Unsightly scratches, marks and small holes in the wood can be filled with dyed shellac or wax as used by furniture restorers. This is applied with a hot knife and then rubbed or sanded to shape.

Dented stocks can sometimes be steamed up again. Soak pieces of cotton cloth in water, fold it into a pad and place over the dent. Using an old dinner knife with a heated blade, press down on the cloth. The water in the cloth boils and the steam is forced into the fibres of the wood. They swell and the dent vanishes (in theory).

Stock finish is a matter of personal choice. If you have been working on a military firearm then a couple of coats of boiled linseed oil will be adequate. If you are going to use the restored antique then varnish may be appropriate. It gives excellent protection but looks unsightly if chipped. I prefer a matt or eggshell finish. Full gloss polyurethane makes a gun stock too shiny for my taste. French polish is ideal for display guns. It is not a durable finish but looks great on something that is not going to get much handling. French polishing is not difficult to master. There are plenty of books and YouTube videos on the subject. Many colleges offer short courses for furniture restorers.

After cleaning the metal parts, give them a coat of conservation grade wax polish. They will not only look great but will be resistant to corrosion and too shiny to gather dust. Reassemble and enjoy!

MARKING AND RECORDING YOUR GUNS

This book is all about the care and maintenance of your guns. I take that to include maintaining ownership. Every time a gun is stolen, the shooting community loses a little bit of its reputation for being responsible. All too often someone who is actually a victim of crime suddenly becomes a criminal themselves in the eyes of the police, even though they are in no way culpable. A detailed description of your guns, together with a note of how you have marked them, will not only give you brownie points in the eyes of the law, but will also go a long way to identifying your property if it is recovered.

If your guns are insured, then your insurers have much less room for contesting any claim you make. Insurance companies are tough and sceptical at the best of times. In times of economic downturn, they become harder than the flint in a musket lock. Equally, if you are to stand any chance of having stolen property recovered then it needs to be both carefully documented and uniquely marked to foil any attempt to sell it on. When my mother's home was burgled, I learnt some hard lessons from that traumatic experience. So that you don't have to learn them,

.320 RF revolver with both paper and electronic records

I've produced some hints about making effective records of your guns and accessories.

We invest a great deal of our hard-earned cash in our hobby so it is common sense to document and mark it properly. I have taken a multi-media approach that combines hi-tech with traditional methods. I've tried to keep things simple, especially where IT is involved. Consequently, I'm confident that anyone can follow this advice and that if the dreaded day ever comes around then you will be well ahead of the game.

Most of us have PCs these days which immediately gives us a powerful tool to create a record of our guns and property using existing database software or, for the more computer literate, one that we have designed ourselves.

Having catalogued thousands of items of arms, armour and militaria, I know the value of a good description. An auctioneer's catalogue entry is his shop window. Similarly, it's your unique written record of your property. A really comprehensive record combines a short narrative description with a more analytical pro-forma type of record which lists dimension, markings and any other unique feature.

For example, take my 16 bore hammer gun; this is how I would describe it.

'A 16 bore hammer-action double-barrelled shotgun, No 123456 by Thomas Mortimer, Edinburgh, c.1885. With Damascus twist 30in barrels, scroll engraved action and locks, Deeley forend catch and walnut stock. The silver escutcheon engraved "JWT". ¼ inch scratch to the left side of the stock.'

There is a great deal of information in those 48 words. Certainly it is enough to confer a certainty of identification, especially as this is a mass-produced object with distinctive marks i.e. serial numbers, in two places. In the case of handmade items, more descriptive phrases are needed, but the principle of listing salient features remains the same.

A description of this type is more than adequate for insurance purposes and for giving to the police.

Having completed the written description, it's time to add pictures. In the age of the digital camera, anyone can take pictures which provide a detailed record of an object's features. Most of us have a good digital camera on our mobile phones so it's very easy to enhance a good written description with some images.

I think it's enough to take wide shots of left side, right side and a view from the top. If you then take a few close ups of things like a serial number, a former owner's initials or a distinctive patch of damage then you have a complete written and visual record.

Shotguns and rifles are best treated in sections of close-ups. For instance, you can take an overall view of your Webley 700, but although it shows what the gun looks like, it can't show that much detail. Take pictures of the lock, the serial number, the butt and the forend.

Having recorded all of this data, bring it together in a computer folder. You can also add scanned-in copies of any supporting documents such as a page from a catalogue, a proof certificate, the vendor's receipt etc. The electronic folder needs to be backed up with a hard copy folder that contains the original documents. It's common sense to store the two well apart so that they cannot both be stolen at the same time.

Similarly, it's vitally important to make a digital backup which also needs to be kept somewhere safe e.g. on a disk in your desk drawer at work, with a friend or family member or in a cloud storage facility. It needs to be easily accessible to add new additions from time to time. It actually takes a good deal of personal discipline to keep files and disks up to date but it is vital to do so. If you are robbed, then the ability to hand the police and your insurance company an electronic record of your property puts you well ahead of the game. The police can circulate the details and the insurance company will know that you are a genuine case because of the excellence of your record keeping.

You have also provided prima facie evidence of lost items. If you provide people with detailed information, they are much more quickly and likely to help you than if you proffer some vague description, written on the back of a cigarette packet.

If you are unfortunate enough to have your property stolen then you can make it hard to dispose of by using a prepared email circulation list of local dealers and auctioneers. The gun trade in Britain is quite small so you can get wide coverage for little effort. Harvesting email addresses is dead easy. The ads in *The Armourer* and other magazines will give you a good start. Build your email group and have a pre-prepared list giving brief details of your property. The first line of the description from your record file is enough. If you list everything you own, then it is a matter of minutes to adjust it to refer to only those items which have been stolen. Attach it to an email giving brief details of the theft plus contact details. When you press the Send button, you have just gone a long way to making your property too hot to handle. As well as making the thieves' lives difficult, self-help that is easy to do is a great morale booster. It makes you feel that you are fighting back and that the odds of some thieving so-and-so's chances of fencing your property have just got very much longer.

So far, I have concentrated on describing property. This is very important but I think it is equally important to mark property as well, particularly if it has few distinctive features. Marked property is also much harder to dispose of. Our charming Community Police Officer recommends writing your name in black felt tip pen on all your garden tools and furniture. That's sound advice but it can't be used for guns because it is not durable. Instead we need to be much craftier in how we mark them.

The great antique gun collector, the late William Keith Neal, always wrote a brief history of every gun he bought on a small piece of paper, rolled it up and popped it into the barrel. The same idea could be applied to your name and address. Once pushed about six inches down the barrel, it is not readily discernible and most thieves would not realise that it was there. This tip is most applicable to muzzle-loading firearms with large bores.

A variation on this theme is to use small self-adhesive address labels stuck under the buttplate and barrel of a long firearm. The gun has to be dismantled to do this. You can also put a label under the grips of most muzzle-loading revolvers. It goes without saying that you should add the locations of these labels to your record file.

More permanent markings can be applied using a fine alcohol-based permanent marker e.g. a CD marker. I know a chap who writes his name and post code in inconspicuous places on the stocks of his rifles and shotguns. I applaud this crafty low-tech marking solution that is difficult to defeat because the marker pen is indelible. Marker pens whose ink shows up under UV light can also be effective if applied to inconspicuous places.

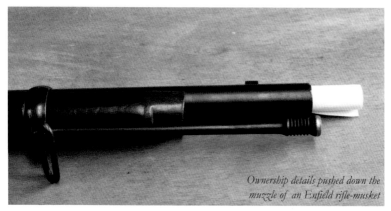

Ownership details pushed down the muzzle of an Enfield rifle-musket

Moving on to more high-tech marking solutions, I am often asked about my views on installing microchips in guns. From time to time some company or other will offer this as a service. While it's excellent for dogs and cats, I believe that it is a complete waste of time for guns and similar objects. I am also uneasy about a private company having a vast database of people's guns. You will get all kinds of assurances that these databases are wholly secure. That needs to be taken with a cellar of salt in light of teenage hackers compromising military and other government databases in recent years.

As far as I'm aware, microchips will not transmit through steel. This limits your choice of installation site to the woodwork. I recall being told by some very pushy man who was flogging microchips and who said he'd had talks with the then Association of Chief Police Officers and that they would be compulsory for every gun in the UK in the next three years. As you might imagine, this cut no ice with me and I rose to his challenge to find the microchip in a shotgun that he brought along. I soon detected a small patch of brown furniture restorer's wax in the heel of the stock. It covered a small hole. I ran a pin punch down the hole, tapped it with a hammer and was rewarded by the sound of glass being crushed. When the gun was scanned, there was no signal from the microchip. Exit pushy salesman with a face like a well-smacked bottom. Microchips are great for pets and big objects like boats and motorbikes. They are useless on guns and other small items with lots of metal in them.

Another high-tech solution that appears to have considerable potential is synthetic DNA or microdot solutions. There are two in the UK – Selecta DNA and Smartwater. They are applied to objects and have a unique code that can be read by the supplier. Consequently, they can be used to identify owners of stolen property. Equally, they can adhere to the clothing of thieves and I am told that they are virtually impossible to remove. As each client has his own unique DNA code, its presence on the clothing of a suspect provides proof of contact with marked property.

Some academic research has been done which suggests that criminals steer clear of these systems if they know they are in use. One study found that 74% of convicted burglars interviewed in prison said that they would not attack a house where synthetic DNA marking was in use. Often a window-sticker is enough to deter an attack. Armed with this knowledge, another friend downloaded the company's logo and made his own window stickers even though he had not bought the

product. His neighbours suffered repeat burglaries while his property remained untouched. I suppose it's a bit like hanging a 'Danger – Mines' sign on a fence around a field. Nobody is going to run across that field to see if you are telling the truth!

These are just a few thoughts on marking and recording your property. You may groan and say that it's a disgrace that this is necessary. I don't disagree with that sentiment but we are where we are. Harsh economic times always lead to increased crime and it makes sense to take enhanced precautions. We now have the added dimension of potential terrorist use of stolen guns.

However, don't forget that marking and recording always need to be combined with good physical security. If a thief can't get at your stuff because your house is well-secured then he can't steal it. In that case he will go and steal from someone else who is not as well prepared. Take the advice of your local crime reduction officer. In my experience, they are eminently sensible people with good practical solutions to the problems that we face. Much useful information about security can be found in the *Firearms Security Handbook* which can be downloaded from the Home Office website.

ANCILLARY EQUIPMENT

Gunslips

A good slip is your gun's first line of protection in the field. It is more than just a device to carry it around in and will go a long way to prevent scratches and dents.

I prefer to use leather or leather-cloth gun slips because they are easier to clean. Mud wipes off easily with a damp cloth and leather balm soon restores the cosmetic appearance. Leather seems to afford better protection, probably because it is tougher than other materials. Give it a going-over with some boot polish occasionally. Fabric slips may be durable and inexpensive but the mud really gets into the weave. It only comes out with a scrubbing brush. In fact, I sometimes throw mine in the washing machine if it is really grim.

If you have been shooting on a really wet day, then do not put your gun in the slip on the way home. Chances are the interior is already wet and you don't want your gun trapped in something which is damp and in contact with the metal. Wet gun slips need to be turned completely inside out and hung up by the strap or loop until dry. Depending of the level of moisture, this may take several days. Laying the slip on the top of a radiator works too. Always be certain that your slip is bone dry before putting your gun back into it.

Occasionally check that the stitching on the suspension is still sound and that the strap and buckle works. You don't want them to fail suddenly and pitch your gun onto a hard surface.

Cartridge belts and bags

Treat these in the same way as you would a gunslip. Cartridge bags often trap rainwater and it is not good for ammunition to be put away wet. Remove the cartridges and stuff the bag with newspaper to dry it out. It will help it to keep its shape too. Don't leave cartridges in the loops of a leather belt. Over time, their brass heads react with the leather to form a green waxy substance called verdigris. The same happens to brass-cased rifle cartridges if left in a leather ammunition wallet.

If you have both a 12 bore and 20 bore gun, only put 12 bore cartridges into the bag. Keep the 20 bores in a belt and only load from that. That way you prevent the possibility of a double load happening. This does not excuse you from looking up the bore of your gun before loading a fresh cartridge but it stops the very dangerous situation of cartridges of different bores getting mixed together.

Ammunition

All ammunition needs looking after if it is to remain reliable. Dry all ammunition thoroughly if it gets wet. These days, shotgun cartridges are made with brass-washed steel heads which are prone to rust. Very light rust can often be rubbed off with a soft cloth. More stubborn patches may need wire wool or a brass bristle brush. Rust is a very hard material and you want to be wary about putting what amounts to an abrasive into the highly polished chamber of your gun. That said, even if a cartridge has a rusty head it is still safe to use if the gun will close on it. However, you may want to keep older ammunition for those occasions where a misfire does not matter, like an informal clay shoot. You do not want a misfire when a really sporting pheasant flies over!

If you are unlucky enough to experience a misfire, keep the muzzles pointing in a safe direction, wait 30 seconds, turn your face away and then open the breech. Dispose of the dud cartridge responsibly.

If you are more of a traditionalist who uses paper-cased cartridges, make sure that they do not get wet and swell. A swollen cartridge will strain your gun's ejectors. You will always notice badly swollen ones, as they won't go in the chamber at all. Never try to force a cartridge into the breech; you may get it stuck halfway and not be able to close your gun. Although a jammed cartridge can easily be removed with a cleaning rod, it may cost you the drive of a lifetime when the sky is black with birds.

Keep ammunition in its packaging until you are ready to use it. An ammunition wallet for rifle cartridges will keep them safe and dry.

Sound moderators

The exterior of a sound moderator needs to be wiped with an oily rag after use. It also needs to be taken off the rifle and allowed to dry, otherwise moisture condenses inside it and causes corrosion which can develop into pinholes in the casing. Remember, a moderator on a Section 1 rifle becomes a firearm in its own right and has to be kept securely when not in use. I can see no objection to it being placed on a radiator to dry in the room that you are in; however if it was still in the airing cupboard a month later, then an offence would have been committed.

Many smaller moderators unscrew to allow the baffles to be lifted out for cleaning. They need to be cleaned using petrol in a well-ventilated area before being wiped with an oily rag and reassembled. Pay particular attention to the screw threads on both rifle and moderator; wipe them carefully to remove any grit or foreign matter.

If you own rifles of different calibres, each with its own moderator, make sure that you don't mix them up. You do not want to fire a .30 cal bullet through a moderator designed for use on a .243 rifle. The result will be both exciting and expensive!

Optics

There is not much to say about optics other than to let them dry out after a soaking to prevent condensation forming inside. They will be more resistant to water if rubbed with a silicone cloth before each outing. Do not be tempted to take one apart; you will never get it back together again.

Make sure all telescopic sight mounts are tight or your rifle will lose its zero. Lenses should only be cleaned with a proper lens cloth; other fabrics or kitchen paper may scratch them.

Knives

My old granny used to say that 'A sharp knife is a safe knife'. A knife whose edge is dull does not cut well and if too much force is applied, it might slip and do you a mischief.

Knife blades need to be kept sharp and free from rust. The hinged joint of a folding knife needs a drop of oil from time to time. Do not be tempted to use the type of sharpener where the blade is pulled against two hard wheels or pieces of metal. These sharpeners remove huge amounts of metal from the blade and eventually destroy the edge. I like the type of sharpener with ceramic rods in a block. They are easy to use and sharpen at the right angle. You can get a knife shaving-sharp with a bit of practice.

Check the sheath regularly to see that it is sound. You do not want a knife in the derriere if the blade goes through rotten stitching when you sit down.

In my estimation one of the best knives is one with a brightly coloured moulded plastic handle. It is hard to lose it and when dirty or bloody it can just go in the dishwasher.

Notes

Notes

Notes

Notes

Notes

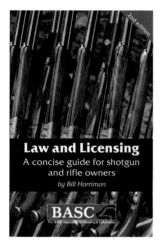

Law and Licensing
Second Edition

9781846892806

A concise guide for shotgun and rifle owners covering all current aspects of firearms law; it is essential reading and provides a point of reference for any gun owner in the UK.

The BASC Handbook
of Shooting

9781846892486

An absolute must for anyone who owns a sporting shotgun; it features both shotgun safety and the basic rules of gun handling, whether in the field, while travelling and at home.

Additional BASC handbooks and sporting books are available from the BASC bookshop – www.bascbookshop.org.uk